Money for Sunsets

2010

Money for Sunsets

Elizabeth J. Colen

Bowling Green, Kentucky
2010

ISBN: 978-0-9824169-3-8

Book design: Jill Runyan
Cover: C.L. Knight

Steel Toe Books
Department of English
Western Kentucky University
1906 College Heights Blvd., #11086
Bowling Green, KY 42101-1086
www.steeltoebooks.com

CONTENTS

refraction,

ACKNOWLEDGEMENTS

I would like to express great appreciation to the editors of the following journals, in which some of these poems originally appeared; sometimes in slightly different versions:

Barn Owl Review: "Dreams of People Waiting in Line"

Bayou: "If Not the Boy"

Chiron Review: "Sandy Hollow, KS" and "Snapshots of Girlfriends"

Exquisite Corpse: "Unsaddled"

Fifth Wednesday Journal: "Slack Tide"

Filter Literary Journal: "Blue #1," "Blue #2," "Des Oeufs" and "Trim"

Knockout: "The First Three Letters," "Fifty Miles of Shoulder," "The Girl in My Basement," "Grand Canyon" and "Portrait of My Mother"

The Normal School: "The Bird Was Not My Sister, But Did Look Like Her"

OCHO #21: "Diving Lessons" and "Matches Between Teeth"

Quiddity International Literary Journal: "What We Look At When We Don't Look At Each Other"

RATTLE: "Aposematic"

Rivet: "January Window"

Silenced Press: "Dislocation Density"

Silk Road: "80 East"

So To Speak: "Iron Jaw" and "The Match"

Spoon River Poetry Review: "Home Before it Divided" and "Waist High By July"

3:AM Magazine: "Survival of the Species" and "After the Fire"

Special thanks to Carol Guess, Francis McNairy, Jean Bos, Louise Bos, Tom C. Hunley, and Kristen Heldmann; and to Bruce Beasley, Kate Beles, Mary Biddinger, Andrea J. Danowski, Oliver de la Paz, Denise Duhamel, Lisa Elliott, Jeremy Halinen, Kate Lebo, Khaled Mattawa, Shane McCrae, Brenda Miller, Suzanne Paola, Deborah Poe, and Sheri Rysdam.

NOTES

Title "The Boredom of Obvious Things" is taken from Czeslaw Milosz's *Road-side Dog.*

"Snapshots of Girlfriends" references the song "Lady Marmalade" performed by LaBelle and written by Bob Crewe and Kenny Nolan.

Title "Saintly Meat of the Heart" is taken from Allen Ginsberg's "Television was a Baby Crawling Toward that Deathchamber."

INTRODUCTION

Although a rabid Twin Peaks fan back in 1990, I always had reservations about the show. What if, in the first episode, the body of an old woman had washed up on the river bank? Or the body of a man? I contend that David Lynch wouldn't have had a series. Laura Palmer, homecoming queen, is, of course, the one to fuel the swirling investigation in the town of Twin Peaks – and to make things even more Lynchian, she's nude and wrapped in plastic.

Flash forward twenty years and we get Elizabeth J. Colen's amazing *Money for Sunsets*. "11 Bang-Bang," the first poem in Colen's remarkable first book, answers the question I posed so many years ago. We get the beach and death, but this time the death is of a "fine-feathered boy made of glass." We get Colen investigating loss, innocence, and violence, drawing on her native Washington state (home of the fictional Twin Peaks.) We get the male gaze refracted and bent and boomeranged back. Though Colen's writing is glorious, the violence itself is not glorified. Colen references white supremacists, bullets, tsunamis, corruption through money, Cambodia, arson, overdevelopment, and abuse – all capturing the creepiness of Twin Peaks, but the wink and nod is gone. Colen's poems look you in the eye.

And speaking of eyes, *Money for Sunsets* utilizes the prose poem, the shape itself suggesting windows and boxes, particularly Pandora's box. Laura Sullivan has written, "Prose poems have a presence you cannot ignore, can't mistake for squeaking floorboards. But the largeness of prose poems is not an obesity, not an excess; every word is muscle." In text blocks, Colen flexes her fabulist muscles, her contemplative muscles, and her neosurrealist muscles. In "January Window," the shower stall becomes a box from which the speaker is forbidden after confronting her lover about the subject of anger. In the haunting "Synthesizer Approximating Strings," Colen is trying to exact a kind of violence, a reenactment of some sort in the backseat of a car in which the speaker admits, "I kept the windows rolled up so no one would stop what I was doing." The car becomes a "casket," another kind of box, a container. Colen's poems are like building blocks, creating an often frightening and sinister structure.

If I were Colen's agent, I'd pitch these poems to a movie producer as "David Lynch meets Gertrude Stein." *Money for Sunsets*, like *Tender Buttons*, is syntactically rich and varied, using fragments, repetition, and word associations. If I were Colen's agent, I might not mention her complicated and smart observations on women, violence, and money – since I'm assuming that most movie producers are capitalists. In "Des Oeufs" Colen writes, "A naked woman as motif is too easy." Too easy, indeed. Innovative and evocative, these poems have arrived at just the right cultural moment. And I, for one, am grateful they're here.

– Denise Duhamel, Judge, 2009 Steel Toe Books Prize in Poetry

Whale of a lie like the hope it was …

—*David Bowie*

For Carol

Your arsenal,

11 BANG-BANG

Box of hair on a beach. Scattered and new, ashes. A fine-feathered boy made of glass. Pin pricks, a hole in the wall. What we thought of that first time came true. Everything all light and darkness. There's nothing that fits outside of good and bad. I came to the war with open arms. I come to you, armless and scarred. What the boy was wearing when he died could fit inside your palm or, if you like, could hang off the two fingers left of your right hand. They wouldn't let us see his face. Scattered and torn, a boy made of glass, shattered. Golden hair pressed into the child's book of verse. Seared locks in a chocolate box, the smell of candy and burn.

SLACK TIDE

You may know this. What is the difference between autopsy and necropsy? A child stares down in anger. The fish follow her home. A whole parade of danger stretches out along the roadway, watching. *I don't believe we've met*, she said. A church walks by. *Saturday*, it says. No one listens. When the body washed up on the beach, no one knew who it was. Police went door to door asking if the residents were missing anyone. *Surely she wasn't one of ours*, they said. In springtime the rains came, the town was sliced open and sluiced, forgotten. The rock fists reigned the beach and stars came out during the day.

MY SUNSET CITY

Clean cut college kids. Utopia of freedom. Utopia of television screen larger than my grandfather's car. Of lax gun laws, large withdrawals, huzzah of lockjaw. Take two boxes, two for the price of no, one. We stray inside the city of sunsets, perilously close. The white supremacist long-distance runner stuffs croissants down the back of his pants. Here we are, alone in the world, getting along in the world. We are not we here. Real world, right here in the palm of my sunset city there are fourteen bullets through a stained glass wall. There are metal fingers digging metal out of dirt, dogs willing bullets out of earth. Dearth of common sense. No fence around a border city. Boys from out of town. Boy's a bad seed. Boy doesn't boy not look like us. The boy does drugs and likes a border town. There's a fence for that, a wall down south. Here we are only bulwark and stockade, blockade and gunpowder. Here we take matters into our own hands.

THE NEXT COLD WAR

Until the empire dies tonight I'll stand here looking at the blue flame in my fake log fireplace. Until the empire ends, the forest floor of my bedroom will criss-cross with snakes of cords. O, my electronics never deceive me. In the information age there's no such thing as boredom. My gas tank is filled with oil, my gas logs: oil, picture frames are wood or oil, but oil was used to make them, and the glass came from somewhere else. They had glass back then. Think industrial revolution, think antique houses and furniture scarred, cleaned up by black soot, diamonds. Everything carbon-based will die, except high-standing politicians buried underground. Mile-deep the mines are digging them. Somebody's got to be left to burn. The walls of my house are painted in oil, all the colors of a modern rainbow, there's brick and turquoise, forest green and cobalt blue, and some yellow chiffon that won't come out of my jeans. Once when I was young my hand stayed stained purple for forty-seven days. No one knew what to make of it. Now I only bruise when you pinch me. You stare at the 3-inch screen screaming independence, screaming free, while I'm stuck to the hood of your car. For good mileage you can never slow down.

WAITING FOR WINTER

If I could have remained all day in the hum of your embrace I would have. I would have in the sick of it stayed. If it could have snowed forever it would have, the flakes lifted themselves off the trees and headed for the hills. In morning white covered the blue. False eyelash legs of spider caught in the dirt trap under your bed. Colony of dried skin and mud flakes when I pulled my panties out. Why don't you clean? You don't have to. The girls come anyway. Did it snow? No. The streets slick with black ice, dry ice in your freezer, fish. Do you see how the clouds stay back? The sun fucks the blue bluer, hazy at the raw helm of light. Good morning, sun. Good morning, cold blue sky. Blue morning, mourning for another breath. Good morning, breath. Do you see the how the white banks against the blue?

JANUARY WINDOW

I had a dream I was lost in your hair. The rain had started, so everything shined. I had started out near your ear, just my mouth on you there, just my tongue creeping up the outside of it, just a little. I know it tickles, so I was hesitant, respectful. You seemed to like it then. You moved against me in that way you know I like. Then I got distracted and found my way into the mess of you. I started at the ear, but I have no idea how I got to where I was, lost. When you're on someone's scalp or the roads of tendrils coming from it, it's so easy to lose your bearings. I know you think, just follow one strand from start to finish, follow it all the way out or all the way to the start of things. But it's not that easy when a girl is lying down. I found myself so close to the way you wash yourself. Your skin was red, raw from rubbing. You clean so well, you shampoo like you're angry. I saw it once, while standing in the shower next to you. You faced the faucet, face in the stream of water, your back to me. I watched the curve of the water from the showerhead fall onto the curve of you, down your back and then I lost it. Your legs are beautiful, but I hardly ever get to them when I look at you. Your fingers were in your hair, like they are now looking for me. When we got into bed, clean and leaving small circles of wet on the sheets, I mentioned the anger I had seen and we never took a shower together again. Sometimes I sit on your couch and think about you in there, what your hands are doing, how strands come away on your fingers.

WE OBEY EVERY OTHER LAW

You remember it later as nothing, a sigh going nowhere. But there in the dark, trees crowding, the windsound through the creek bed took you away from yourself. And you, then as now nothing but fear shouldered over, a pair of long legs, a pretty face, your forehead hit a branch, and you left the forest scarred. I could find you by the rough line anywhere. And now, with the low sun silvering the mud halfway out the bay, you say, *I had a dream it was like this once,* yet when I ask what *it* was you say nothing and only stare. Your face is tilted. I like you better when you're sideways, I want to say, I like you best at horizontal. I watch you while you take stock of birds in the park, black oystercatcher, marbled godwit, gulls. *I'm different now,* is all you say. We hear then see a plane over the trees, lifting off, a scatter of sparrows. Later, in the car, you draw pictures in my hand.

THE RULES OF SUBDUCTION

Read about tsunamis from a thick blue book. Read about the Big Ones, the ones that killed, the causes, how many dead. Read about velocity and volume, then go down to the water. Walk the beach, feet tipped in low waves. Imagine every tremor an earthquake — waves, birds beating quiet wings, a waterfall — then shiver as you watch the horizon for the swell.

Find what could have been shell shards or the bones of human fingers — carpal, metacarpal, phalanges. Leave them at the water, untouched by the stick in your hand. The birds caw absently, disinterested, even the gulls who peck at plastic in the parking lot.

Later, you will be unable to sleep, remembering those bones, the wet white, the sand still in the just before.

DIVING LESSONS

You longed for that perfect affliction, the one you didn't see in yourself. Blind and rattling through the undergrowth, a ground vole comes up for air. You choke too to see the earth against his face, soot-covered nose, eyes sewn over. You thought once of being an astronaut, a pilot, deep-sea diver, or if nothing else a shipwrecked mess left. You thought some distance from the ground zero of it all would do you good. But once you left dirt, the muscle of your lungs stopped. In the hum of twin engines, the thin air made you bleed, blood-shot, your head thrown back. In the quiet of the ocean, like the violence of the dance floor, you feared the dark of every passing body. Fin slash or shirts opened like knife cuts from throat to navel. The turned up image of yourself in the bottom of the glass. Remember to breathe.

THE BOREDOM OF OBVIOUS THINGS

She was in love with the doorbell, but you loved the door. She was in love with the piano, but you liked black notes on white paper, especially when you set the paper on fire. She was in love with two hands, but you were in love with the tightrope, toes like a fist on a forethought of wire. You were in love with paper; isn't that what everyone said? On fire — her hands at the keyboard, soundtrack to your exits and entrances. I was a footnote in a second-rate orchestra. I was god in a minor religion, scattering Post-Its instead of scattering seeds.

THE SPEED LIMIT OF STITCHES

Small children explaining exhaust me. I stepped away from the curb. The graffitied post broke the sunrise in two. Mechanical thud of the light changing, machine in a bright yellow box. I clapped. There was handholding, but my hands were free. I tensed in anticipation or vicariously, wet palmed when my hands left each other after the last slap. We didn't know the streetcar we met, you didn't warn the child. Mother hovered at the side of the road, dialing. Nobody else had a phone and she was on hold. The pock-marked asphalt greyed with ice, the way snow turns from wonder to blow.

IRON JAW

Behind the coffee shop, you swing by your teeth from a gold trapeze. No, this isn't metaphor. There is a bright bar held by thick wrists of nylon I can't see the end to. Stage lights dot the crowd, small shadows in the art of forgetting. Children held in the air by children writhe, sharp-fisted, many-headed offerings to the sway. Big circle of light like everything you wanted remains trained on you. You have a girlfriend named Zeke I don't understand. No, Zeke speaks quite clearly. It's the facial hair that does me in. The deep voice. The baritone. The adjusting of the crotch from time to time. Zeke and I sit down below. Zeke and I walk into a bar. No, a brick-lined alley, a circus tent. This could be a tent. The glint from the bar makes Zeke's hair seem unreal. Zeke and I walk into the bar of the striped tent while the bent pins of your legs thrash, while the slow blue snow of your eye shadow drops over the crowd. Zeke buys me a beer and I say, no you don't get to do that. Chivalry of the dead sex. What's inside your pants? I reach between your girlfriend's knees not because I want to, but because of the memory of you kneeling on the sidewalk in front of me, your skirt hiked up to your chest and the pee running out of you. You dragged me to the bathroom, dragged a finger of hand soap over your teeth and called it brushing. I pressed you, the smell of piss and perfume against the wall. When we kissed we frothed like abandoned rabid animals.

UNSADDLED

Goodbye, Deborah had said after the third long goodbye. This fourth would stick, she thought. Fist in hand. He could not keep from leaving her. By leaving I do not mean leaving, I mean only that he saw other girls.

He had paused then and looked at her like horses do, that slightly sideways angle of the head, dark, open eyes blinking only when they have to, afraid they'll miss something or be sideswiped somehow if they don't stay trained on the object at hand.

In hand, a rock, the shards of glass surround. They would have had much, but they would never have had language between them. Star dark inside the living room, torn curtain (but that's how it's always been), the broken window. When she looked out the new round flaw in the living room's large pane, the wind whistling through and the cat whining from the floor, when she looked out she heard the stop and start static of retreat, felt the warmth of hidden anger, the grey orb of shadow creeping over trees. The beach wanted her so bad, sand kicked in from the coast, roiling on the wave of wind through the maw. When I say sand, I mean every sense she'd ever had came back to her. His willing hands, his grand mouth, the way he spoke and said nothing at all, the moan, the deep-throated grunts, his bowlegs. When I say sense I guess I mean the gritty way she loved him. His ass in profile, his round, hard ass then cradled in her hands.

Another stone sailed through, a descended angle. The cat scattered. The round shadow grew, the blowtorch static grew, her love, a bright balloon on the front lawn of everything she'd ever let go of. She let go of the gun in her hand, pulled the hair out of her mouth. His horse eyes. She would never forget how she put her fingers right through the black of his pupils, fingered the soft mass behind and found girl parts, arms and legs, ears, breasts, feet, belly, bottom, brunettes and blondes, and found his fingers on them. Worse, the open palms of his hands, his lifeline sliding over. His flesh was warm, skin thick, the jelly of his eyes came away in her hands. She wiped them on her jeans. Jelly eyes, horse eyes. Skin thick. A neigh. Cheap mane, a bad haircut. A boy, a horse. Girl parts. A braided tail.

Deborah brushed the sand from her face, took a last look at the putrefying horse, and stepped into the hot-air balloon forever.

BETTER METHODS TO EXPANDING THE UNIVERSE

Joy is running a meat market in Stockton. Low lights and mood music, rude hands probe bellies exposed in bitter fashion cold to wind in portside town. Revved-up engine, boy at idle, grease the idol, and crease the sheets so they hold you better. Repeated speaking patterns streamline imperfect practice, the less-than-deft exchange of hands, eyes sway, hair a mussed mess, toothbrush on the floor, fingers wet with what, blue goo of clean across the gums and watered down with time held against the bathroom door. The what-am-I-doing-here mirror glance, the search for unseen comb, rooting through the space behind the glass-backed cabinet, amber silos of pills and an arsenal of tweezers stock the shelves against ticking need. Car parked outside welcome to the god of you in leather seat, guided home by electric sun repeated in streetlamps flickering off in the first blue light and shadows of the note you left behind.

INTERSTITIAL DEPLOYMENT

What she wants she can't get. Video blossoms on pink. On dogwood. On downtown striptease. Empty or invisible boats to line the docks, make water matter in this time of evaporation, this time of liquid finding no level, of liquid going elsewhere. Blood liquid on timetable corpse with limpid flowers lining the box. Elder wood on curled wood floor, sensing necrophilia or Cambodia or ill at ease. I'll line them up. She snakes coy glances around the dance floor. Remembers the faces of the already spun. He wakes late, gets there late. He was never asleep, his backside so overwhelmed by the sheet shaking off. We were never so stable, never so chair. We went where it happened. We wanted what we got.

SYNTHESIZER APPROXIMATING STRINGS

I paid her $40 to lie in the back seat of my car. I put my hand over her mouth, pretended it was your mouth, your warm tongue. "Stop that," I said. I could feel her lipstick adhering to my palm, the hot breath from her nose, the wet air inside her mouth keeping it from caking. And then the sweat. I kept the windows rolled up so no one would stop what I was doing. I looked at her. While the quantity of parts was just the same — one mouth, two eyes, eyelids tearing, two ears with color hanging, shoulders, breasts and waist, two arms held by her side, fingers curled and grabbing, two legs and a cunt between them, feet I could not see in her shoes — she was nothing like you. I longed for your teeth, to holler "fuck you" into your hair. Her smell was not the same. It walled up between us in the enclosed casket of my car. Her legs angled against the doorjamb and squeaked when she moved. "No," I said. She said I could have just told her to be quiet, just asked her to hold still. But that wasn't the point to any of this.

BLUE

She planned for a second coat of blue, but looked good standing there as she was. The earrings hung down from her head like the snapped branch that dug into the house after the storm. I thought she had blood on her neck and she laughed, wiping something away and never letting on what it was. "Why do you do this to me?" she said. "Why do you turn on the news as though nothing has happened right here?"

BLUE

Paint blocked our way out of the room. Fire tore through the hall, we could hear it beating against the walls like a million moths' papery wings. Smoke sifted in through the space under the door, through the cracks in the jamb and I thought of your smoke rings. And how never once as I watched those impeccable O's had I ever imagined something like this: feeling the heat on the bedroom walls, choking from smoke in the room, shaking the window like that last can of paint, cursing the second coat of blue.

THE PERFECT DECEMBER

I wanted to believe it was true. That green bells ring loudest, the copper cracking to rust. I wanted to hear when he found her like that. The hollering his mother said would never end. She stood in the doorway in tears. The sound seems hollow with only the memory of sound. *What happened to description?* the smallest boy asked. He stared at the church and wanted it to reveal itself. It wandered away. Someone passing said, *we had a month of Tuesdays once. We were never forgiven.*

MONEY FOR SUNSETS

A visible red line moved along the horizon and we thought it was the end. You grabbed rocks to fill your pockets in case it came to that. You imagined wild dogs and truculent boys. Your jacket became bulky. I thought better of it, thought less weight the way to go, in case the water rose. You climbed on the old pier, the more rickety to highlight to end of all. The wind picked up. The seagulls played with it, unflappable and grey in the last light. You were black against the red. I could not see your eyes. You said, "I'd like to thank the academy," and jumped off into the waves.

TAKE

Shot. Sit. Before her. In the abandoned train car. Lenses almost singular, cameras aimed close, capture nothing. Smell her breath, taste the way her tongue could taste, tasting yours, mint. Sweet, slow sound, her jaw rounding out the silence. Do not speak into the quiet, do not speak into her wintery mouth, those lips ice poles to stick a tongue to, frozen, schoolyard charms and incompletes. "Closer," he says, the reason for our mid-pose, frozen glare. "Closer," he says, "I want you in profile." Laugh. Not long, not really. "I want you," he says, moves, "now, here." Move closer. "Look at each other. Now, look." Glance everywhere, the car's rust roof, floorboards stumbling, trackshine below from the sun coming in, burst cushions the color of mustard or phlegm. "Look," he says, camera poised, "now, look." A look, click, shot, contained. Look away, lock legs in leaving. Stumble out the unhinged door you came in.

COASTERS

In a best-selling mood today, you drank me under the table. Your change rattled like chains under the table. Our card game resembles a dogfight on mute. We can't meet at home. You lay down a five, ask, do you really need to know what he said to me. We went to a karaoke bar once where a man stood on the stump of stage and while the intro to Neil Diamond's *Forever in Blue Jeans* played, he asked the audience, can you hear me in the back. He was kidding, but everyone nodded, yes. He smiled at his joke and we smiled because we alone had not said yes or nodded. We were in the back with our hands in each other's hair, tucked around forever. When you ask, do you really need to know what happened, I don't know what you mean. Nothing, I thought. Then said nothing. You've always had hubcap eyes. What I mean to say is you're leaving now. Your chin points nowhere. Your mouth. Your nose is a symptom of the flu, like muscle aches and the quick onset of fever. What I mean to say is that your scarf got caught in the door and rather than strangle you it fell off without your notice or you let it go simply not to open the door again to alert me to your failure. I gathered composure and coasters for kindling, lit two matches before the third one took and burned you from memory.

FIFTY MILES OF SHOULDER

After the rain, we quickly lost interest in what we went there for. The ground steamed, seemed to swell at the base of trees, of breathing, your throat next to mine. You seemed fine to call it all off. The nick on your cheek had dried in a line. I held your hand. I emptied the Coke can into the brush. You started off softly about where this was going. I was fifty miles of highway, wet in stripes from the way traffic works. I was fifty miles of shoulder. I was stars of glass from broken bottles. I was a whole empty bottle of beer and strips of cloth that could have been anything once. I was the cracked paint that ran parallel, the lines that marked me. I was the sporadic glow of exit signs and the grey leading away from the road. I was the dirty grass. I was the styrofoam, the used condoms snaked in dirt, the cigarette butts. I was not the overpass or the horse standing off in the field. I was the bad mow job when the workers got lazy. There were parts of me springing up everywhere, waist high to the man walking me. I was the man you picked up, the one who worried us both.

the silence,

COUNTING

A child wakes up laughing. Sheche sheep fetish in her hand, bottled water on her nightstand. Mother's been gone all night. Somewhere in the yard the laughter fades. It cannot be heard from the street.

A man dreams of stage fright. Of being sawed in half is not so scary as the faces looking on. He wakes in wet. The night surrounds the key card in his mouth, to what hotel, teeth chattering beat a plastic staccato.

A woman wakes at her front door, turning the knob into nothing. She laughs and goes back to bed.

UP THEN DOWN

I didn't wake when you stood over me, blocked out the sun. I was dreaming of horses and you fit the profile. Staggeringly tall, but willing to be mounted. One tug of your hair and you're off. I remember the time you handed me a water glass that tasted like fire. We got drunk on whiskey and whispers. Your father made you walk down the stairs until you got it right. I stood holding your sandwich, the dressing of which melted into the bag in the shape of Australia. "I'll never get out of here," you said. But you did.

AMERICAN BEACH

The ocean is deep green. Gulls flock like plastic bags against the clouds, caw. Against the tide. Wet beach, post-storm, hold feet like sweaty palms of not yet. Here, before the Ritz there were beach shacks, clapboard siding, paint sanded off by sand. Before the shacks there were more dunes than lovers, seaspray and grit in various hair. When I was small, I set fires here, leaves and brown things that washed up on the shore. Toenails and jellyfish entrails, hair I shaved from our legs I saved to watch the crisp sparkle and burnsmell. I torched pictures, newspapers, letters, and boys. Seaweed scorched like sex smell, more organic than fingers knotted inside. When I was small, I lost everything here, clapboard walls scratched with sand. Too eager the wind. The deep green eyes. Flames licked black smoke as we tossed the condom in and sucked in our little children, the ones, white, the night withered away. What saved us melted. We felt so adult. It only hurt when he stopped. Boy made of sand. He only stopped when I hit him. Boy made of boy. He only stopped with the tide, frozen mid-ebb that day. The sea softens the castle spires we made, legs lock like bulkheads, and hotels stand as monuments to what we haven't yet destroyed.

LATCHKEY

In the place with the two dogs, two compost bins guard the back wall. A truck spins wheels in the alley. The mud was driven down there in the last downpour. We watch the cabin next door for signs of life. Danny sounds words like *shark* and *necklace* while they swim by on the silent screen. We don't like weaponry, but hold butter knives to Dolly's head in hopes for something better. Sunshine blinds those who go outside.

We were magic then. The deckchairs enveloped our invisible charm. We were that way at sunset and all through the night, although at first I worried the night might be dead. We took the lapping of waves as our heartbeats, wet and salty and too far away. We were that way through the dawn, red on our terrible faces. Something always happens to lovers like us. The wooden chairs left stripes on our thighs. I wanted to write something on you. Then the rain came and we were one with the sea, charmless and vacant when the ship finally docked.

SURVIVAL OF THE SPECIES

If I knew my mother would slap me for saying she married for money, I would have done it sooner. The red hand on my cheek speaks of love. The mirror smiles and caresses. I look just like her. If I had known my father, I would have said anything to get his attention. But the wind warps the trees so that the ground has that warmsick staticky feel. The way the sunlight comes through the leaves, when the leaves move. It's unfair to think of darkness on a day like today, even when the sun leaves. If my mother knew I liked women the way she likes men, she would have hung me. My brother likes women too. The Bible says he is O.K. My sister so far likes small dogs and singing hymns. My brother swings from the garage. My brother breaks the beam.

AFTER THE FIRE

When I was seven my mother was pregnant with you. I remember she was sad for a time, saw no one, did not answer the door, the phone, did not open mail. The doors all clicked when they shut. She locked herself in the bedroom we shared. We had moved back home to her parents again. I only knew she was pregnant later, when her stomach pushed out of her size 4 jeans. Then I remembered the sadness. One day mother stood against the wall. I found her there, holding the doorjamb, her head down, breathing hard. She said, "get the doctor." I didn't know what she meant. "I'm seven," I said. She told me I was insolent. I didn't know what that meant either. When her mother came home they drove away in the van. That night I dreamt she came home with no belly, no you. Her stomach was flat like before when I used to push the round of my fatness into last year's tiny pants. The waistband left a red line around my middle like I'd been cut in two. I was always growing and she stayed the same, except for you babies. In the dream she held a rock the size of a grownup's fist and said it was what she had carried inside. Sans baby she seemed more content. She was back to size 4. She smoked cigarette after cigarette. No one hit anyone. The rock was shiny and you. I was so happy I ran through the house with a box full of matches. And then you arrived three months later, a month after the wedding, long after the fire.

FLOOD PLAIN

She was in love with the doorbell, the men who came, the orange blossom scent the porch gave off when she reached to get the mail. The car out front leaked oil and the pavement, which leaned into the curb, was split by this thin blackness like the steep creek bed dividing us from town. The street would be clean soon. The street would be wide with water. She found a funnel under the stairs, where the soil had leached out. She found an old plastic bag wrapped around the clapping sound her hands made slapping back. Everything was busy. We had no time for fishing, reels, we had no time for dancing. We were so hungry then, our calluses yielding to yellowed teeth, nails coming off in the water. On the other side of the galaxy her hands flooded the keys. At nine the men came with water. At nine she washed her hair. I stood against the wall, pleased at the tapping, pleased at the tightening wires, pleased at all the wet.

FOR NINETY YEARS, A DIAGRAM

I don't know anyone born in 1919. My great grandmother died long ago. There's a threshold between my house and the outside world that's been crumbling for years. Gateway to the wind whistle, riverboat of wood from here to there. The ants ride in, drawn by the peanut butter on the dog bone, the water by the door. Some say winged creatures are souls returning, visiting. I say hello like I know a butterfly or sparrow, but I want them to have their own lives.

When I was a child there were cracks in my grandmother's house, like the ground shifted and the house gave up holding on. In the morning I waited until the sun hit the slice in the bedroom ceiling. Sometimes I watched the birds fly by, quick flit of blackness breaking up the blue.

THE BIRD WAS NOT MY SISTER, BUT DID LOOK LIKE HER

The book smelled like smoke when she gave it to me, prompting me to sneeze. Gulls lined the highway, walked smack into cars stalled on the shoulder. I'd never seen anything like it. Movement was halted by the desire of the girl on the overpass. She had wings in her hair and no one knew where they came from. When she'd tried to fly it hadn't worked and so here we were again trying to parse atmospheric pressure from lift. Trying to make a life out of nothing but air. We went home again, but no one was there. We lined up on the stage my sister had built in the basement to put on Molière once she'd decided what a misanthrope was. We lined up along the stage, then walked three steps stage right, turned toward front again. It was a cold night and the basement heater only heated the stairs. We held unlit cigarettes to our lips, then let the V of our fingers pull them away.

IF NOT THE BOY

Riff-raff, the broken ax, passenger side window scratched with something, bottle top hopping and sleep sleeping until tomorrow. I stop home for clothes. My mother, god love her, says we dress like sleeping bags. I rip another hole in my jeans for life or skin to spill out of. The sometimes too-much heat beats my knees and causes stumbling. Ever after do I take this boy to me, if not the boy then the memories. What lasts lasts at last. Ever after. The boy with the wild blue eyes gives a tab, I tongue it. We give ourselves burns on my pink synthetic carpet while listening to Billy Joel. We sing Allentown like our throats burn from ashen steel town air and impending unemployment. Upstairs my mother has become an endtable. Her eyes are. Her teeth are, though not smiling, are. Her hands and nails are. Her hips and lips. Her knuckles and nose are. Her face altogether is is is. And her legs are legs. At last they are nothing but legs.

PORTRAIT OF MY MOTHER

A sketch of my mother's face gives good impression of the woman within. Drawn in brown crayon, the eyes are flat, sight obscured going both in and out. The lids in blue, heavy, require the uplift of beige feathered lashes to keep them aloft. The skin is pink, shaded grey along the contours, not for wrinkling — that onslaught of time against elasticity and slenderness of pores — but for the haze of smoke rising from the slim cigarette just below the picture's lowest border. The mouth is a red cut across the paper never gotten quite right. Her ears are hidden in her hair, which sits on the oblong orb of her head in curled clumps that resemble cross-sections of tumbleweed more than anything living or dead. From the black tip of the collar one gets a sense of her dress, simple, elegant. In a word, devastating. The neck that emerges is graceful and shows little wear.

SANDY HOLLOW, KS

The way he looked at me and she looked away. The pitcher just out of reach, my small hands spilling the milk. The milk on the table. The milk in my hair. The sound of the TV on mute. The sound of the TV up loud. My brother and I crushed a turtle in the creek bed, startled the life out of a black cat that had crossed our path. The hum of the holler speeded up. The yellow van did not slow for the quick crossing. Clouds lifted out of it, hung in the air. I lit my hair and listened to the sizzle twice, head underwater, the nation going away. Crisis passing. Sparklers in May, June, July. The kids across the street just stared. No one had to warn them away. Pinches of sand sold, the dry dirt blowing into our hair. Handfuls sealed in small plastic bags, call it rock crystals, call it diamonds, cocaine when we knew what that was. Frog legs in buckets, strands of our hair.

WAIST HIGH BY JULY

The cornfields a blur in green, knee high by July. Somewhere between the feet and heart the green grows. Somewhere between waking and sleeping is the hot side of the car, my face pressed into the glass. And also me above the asphalt, floating alongside. I am always sitting with my mouth open. I am always flying by. Other kids remain convinced of my dumb numbness. Even my brother calls me slow. Kids play keepaway with my report card. One shouts, *I thought she was retarded.* But somewhere between sleeping and waking, mom or dad driving, car speeding away from somewhere at sixtyfive, seventyfive, body hinging on body, body in singular, body in double, troubled. Here in the car, here along the road, speed of light off the window, sun in my eye. What did she think I would do when she took her pants off? I panicked. She had a boyfriend then, but that hardly stopped the winding back and letting go. The metal spinning toy of me. She knew what she was doing. Somewhere between the glass and me. Somewhere between the third glass of Cherokee Red, pink circles drying on the table. Somewhere between the pillow and the ceiling, a body in double, single mind, single mine. What would I do with a mouth full of leg? Sun set and I went blind. Sunset, a blur in red, waist high by July.

A PASSING NOTE

The inked-in edge of the paper folded over, thumbprint in duplicate, triplicate, quadruplicate. Glacial striations and whorls of hourly announcements over the PA, hourly hounds of the brain-scraping bell. Carbon copy times, ditto dried and blue wore off against the new black asphalt steaming and the too-clean reflection of fluorescently ticking halls. I met you by the river, no, stream. I met you in your mother's leather jacket, swung down and gathered stones. The sidewalk home washed with the indigo sorrow of curfew. Dinner ate dinner and the stones rumbled from the inside, great caws of disturbed laughter as they locked together. The sidewalk consumed itself, penned a few paragraphs about decay, made copies and passed them to all the stone slabs waiting patiently behind.

SNAPSHOTS OF GIRLFRIENDS

Junior high French class was the first time pre-marital sex crossed my mind. I thought it was a new thing. I contemplated how my grandparents' generation and beyond had practiced great restraint. No one had babies out of wedlock. There were no bastard grandparents that I'd ever heard of, and abortion didn't exist until the 70s when everything sexy came unhinged. That we watched *Manon des sources* that day seems irrelevant. I don't remember any sex in that at all. I pressed my legs together gently, then harder. Then, noting the darkness and that no one could likely see me, I kept up with the motion. Slow and hard, my Chuck Taylors squeaking lightly as I pivoted my feet. Spinning through my head while I watched a French girl run through French weeds in a French field was the refrain from a disco tune. *Voulez-vous coucher avec moi ce soir*? I liked the pause between *ce soir* and the rest of the question. Urgency in afterthought. Not *voulez-vous coucher avec moi* sometime next week or ever, but will you do it now? I wondered what it would take to get from age 13 to a place where a sentence like that in French or any language would work. I sang it to my dog, because she alone would never ask what I meant. I sang it to the pictures on my wall of Matt Dillon and C. Thomas Howell and the two Coreys, of course. I sang it to the half-inch picture in the yearbook of Tommy McGrath. And to the snapshots of girlfriends I kept under my pillow.

THE FIRST THREE LETTERS

She wanted me to memorize her name. I told her I'd rather have her number so I can call and leave messages. Let's start with the alphabet, she said. First letter. What I didn't say is that the mole is all she'll leave behind. Dark white behind my irises, a memory in negative. There's a whole ocean behind that spot and she's making out letters on the page, she's watching them appear. Her name could be anything, I don't trust her. Her face rusts in my hands. She tears up, not knowing what I want. I tell her I don't want the alphabet. The sheets are stained with ice cream. We're unfed and the dog who was licking the floor just a minute ago is now pulling the door open with a paw. It goes scratch scratch. We both know what it is, but we turn to look so we don't have to look at each other.

THE GIRL IN MY BASEMENT

The girl in my basement is all sound. I wish for our sakes she were more movement and less mouth, more arms, less fingers, more red and less blue. The girl in my basement makes faces into my palm when I quiet her. She says love should be noisy. I say there's a time because we both know anyplace is good for love. I say there's a time because we — sixteen and fifteen — aren't in it. The sound of my brother back from soccer, his cleats hit his bedroom door, he clears his throat, coughs and spits into something. The sound of my sister sleeping in her crib is the sound of static on the monitor coming through the floor. We hear everything the everything is so thin. The sound of my mother making meatballs isn't so much a sound, but a feeling of pink meat matted and the smell of oregano, then finally the sizzle of the pan and my mother masticating a bit of raw. The girl in the basement is all ears when I tell her what her cunt tastes like. She giggles when I talk about the vise of her legs, thighs pressing my cheeks. It's the only way it works, she says. It's the only way. I allow the laughter, but when she sounds like a ghost again I smash her face into the wall. She likes this, likes the cool texture of wood paneling and the lines it leaves in her skin.

HOME BEFORE IT DIVIDED

Home before it divided. Before baby and after. Not baby. Before Daddy's slap. Then. The reddened years of my face. Before the woods and after. After the moon canal cuts of my legs. Before the adults and after the children. Before seatbelts. And me in between.

The smell of a man, repeated in his son.

Before the funeral, you smell like your father. After ever after. The absence of boy or man. The scent of a hand. Hand washing itself. Before the rain and after the rain. Lawn sodden. The walk pooled, reflecting the sky. After the storm. After the grey. After the grey.

BECAUSE OF THE SUN SHE NEVER CAME IN WINTER

No one did the dishes. Nobody cooked at all, so everything stacked in the sink was all glasses, bowls, and spoons, and the odd clump of cereal congealed in the rusted mouth of drain. Nobody cooked, but terror came cheap by the pound and ready to eat. When grandmother came we were on the mend. The other fifty-one weeks no one looked back, no one lifted the shades.

FIRST RIGHTS

For the girl I no longer love who lies in the grass, her blanket ironing down the green. For the rock paper scissors that divided day into night and the spun bottle that figured out more than we knew. I watched her body become an arc, feet tensed in the coiled sense of longing. That we had each other was always so wrong. Locker slammed, damns from her Mom, the boys gathering round. Fist inside her, everything warm. The way she cried with her face down on the damp sheets or the cold floor, the way my arm draped over the back of her neck. If I pulled her hair, it was only to say I love you into her ear. If I held my hand on her back, it was only to make her stop moving so much. I never cut her. I never once told her she was wrong.

DREAMS OF PEOPLE WAITING IN LINE

I lived on the back gate. Watched cars go by and once a day the mail truck with its rolling door clattering over the ruts in the road. Watched the neighbor's yard run thin through the bushes and rows of bright flowers besotted with bees. Watched the three green children rocking the sand, mowing the grass with their hands. Their eyes saluted planes that flew by, though it wasn't clear they knew what they saw. *Rugby knees*, my father said when I came home bruised. *What have you been doing?* I thought about the bark scalping, thought about the toads in the yard. I told him I'd been planning a bank heist and he laughed at me. I hid the money under the stairs.

THE MATCH

As I am not in favor of a racket, I move away from barking dogs, crying children, and drums. Not trusting most silence, I move away also from dogs that may bark, children with faces screwed up in the art of the almost tear, and all drums, whether or not they are inhabited by drummers or other people with sticks. I jump at loud noises and soft ones. I jump when you open the gate, I jump when you approach the gate. I do not notice airplanes, they are either too far away or impossible to miss. Art museums, while supposedly quiet, are sometimes teeming. Stand in front of any Caravaggio and listen to the paint squeak, watch light move intrepidly humming as it sweeps across a face or a landscape, and witness each subject shriek about his or her death, murdered or not.

refraction,

DES OEUFS

A naked woman as motif is too easy. Breasts are universal. Life, birth, blood, and all of that. I see you standing against the wall of a French patisserie thinking, I will never see you standing against the wall in a French patisserie again. The plane will go down and all the croissants inside us, chocolate and buttered and otherwise, will go down too. I want to explain the laws of motion to you, but when you're standing against a wall it seems silly to imagine you rocking your fingers inside me. It seems silly to imagine the pleasure you will try to give me later in the hotel room. La chambre d'hotel. We will wake up way too late to really see anything at the Louvre but the crowded Mona Lisa and maybe Venus de Milo from the stairs. We will put on clothes. We will have eggs for breakfast, but they will call them something else.

TRIM

Sometimes I feel nostalgic about your dark mouth, the way things disappeared in there. I could be silent or I could speak and watch as my words dissolved, which amounted to almost the same. Sometimes I heard the start of the word I had spoken: *confused* became *con*; *whipped cream* became *whip* became *wh*, just a whir. *Bedroom* became just a *bed*, became *be*, which is where we existed. *Reno* became *re*, became do it again. *I can't believe we got married*, I thought, but you said it. If I'd brought it up it would have been *mar*. And your fingernails when they dug into my wrists were impeccably clean. I wanted to say you were reckless, you were feckless, but this became wreck me and fuck me. When I said I was wary it came out as war.

WHAT WE LOOK AT WHEN WE DON'T LOOK AT EACH OTHER

Lotion on plump hands, the fingers caress each other like lovers. Small child scowls against an unwilling chest, beating for beating. Another man with a beard like your father's turns the corner into our view. What shape will he take? The tilted table, wilted dahlia getting nothing from the jar. The still fan, the exposed pipes along the ceiling, a simple subway map. Not at all like that time in Paris you cried on the Metro stairs. We were girls then. You were too much for me. We found Jim Morrison's grave easily, followed the pot smoke and graffiti, left cigarette butts and a lock of your hair. We found Proust only by sheer force of my will. There's a way we'll never be that full again. The noxious bar smell crawling up the walls, the lights on wet pavement, and your skinned knee, insistence on cabs. The throat you held against the wall. *Jamais*, you said, *jamais*. Hours to parse out newspaper headlines, the mountains of foam, good shoes in room after room, the way you loved me.

OOLONG

A famine. You, me. On the brink of war, a teapot set on the table's edge, spout-side out. A hovering. I watch the steam rise between us, watch the way it mutes the color of your shirt, your waving hands. I try to focus on the cause of the day, anxiety or retribution, what words your hands carve out. But can't. I'm wondering, in all of this — your face, your hands, hunger in Africa and here, war in the Middle East and here, you and I here and there — if enough steam leaves will the pot unbalance enough to fall.

SURSUM CORDA

We're at 33 thousand feet. A woman walks by with wings in her hair. We're too close to heaven for angels. The man in 21D has a band around his arm tied tight, its leather glistening in the half-light from the bulb at his ear. A plane in the dark is a bedtime in motion. Each traveler remembers a lover's warm breath, the even sound of the clock in the kitchen, the troubled latch digging into the gate's wood, whistling wind. Each passenger cocooned in silence, loud as death's sullen embrace.

RAINED OUT

You invent someone to take the fall for you. Black ball on the horizon. Black and tall and still as water. You invent someone to fall for you. Over and over, eyes meet across a crowded room and Wham-Boom hors d'oeuvres severed, the wedding is rained out again. This time he picks up his clothes, leaves a message in the laundry room made of socks and neckties. *Went out. Back soon. Don't wait up.* You invent someone to follow you. The stalking started long ago you tell the women at the gym. And what does he look like? they ask. Tall, black with a sway back that walks when you run.

80 EAST

Forty more miles of Idaho, the sun hangs low in the rearview, riding like ball-lightning on an eighteen-wheeler. You've been sleeping since Salt Lake — crescent lashes rimming your lids below the Ray Bans you refused me when I took over the wheel. I squinted from the bones of light sliced off passing cars' chrome. You said you'd take the blame if we became wreckage on the plains.

While you sleep I think of your mother leaving five year old you on the train outside of Warminster. She stood on the platform, pulling air through a Pall Mall, watching your sunburned head, sweat-wrecked hair forming a halo against the glass. You always forget she broke both heels running as the train pulled away, her cigarette unstubbed, burning full moon into her wrist as she fell.

Night falls as two cupped hands over the eyes. Idaho is a memory of rotting. Wyoming paces back and forth along the highway, dark fields and nothing and more dark fields. And that flick-flickering of lane lines shoot past like stars.

When you wake I'll be pulling in to a Motel 6 or 8 or Holiday or Budget Inn. Sheets stained before we stain them, red of bedbug-itch, unplastered gashes in bathroom walls the night wants in. I'll be pulling in under neon-gaudy signs for Breakfast Bars and Free HBO, and you'll barely open your eyes to tell me it's too early to stop. When I come out of that office with diamond-shaped keychain you'll look at me as though it's been years.

CRAVE

I went to Warm Springs for the water, but heard nothing but the chugging of machinery lifting stone slabs out of rot. So I went to Atlanta for a fix, Jacksonville for a fix, all the way to Miami for a fix, then to Nashville. I went until I could not feel my foot on the gas, my thighs against the vinyl seat, sweating. I went until I could not see the road. I went down on a dozen girls in a dozen bars and can't remember a thing about the angles. Skirted leg under my arm or over my shoulder, leaned back against a mirror dirty with lipstick phrases and grease-pencil pleas to God. The noise in the other room, every other room, is a bass thump, a beat we can move to. She gathers up my hair and breathes into the memory of a hot faucet, steam bath, the natural way the water moved. She thinks about her uncle's polio and how it never went away. And all those long days riding shotgun on his lap, catching air as uncle rode the ramp into the garage.

DISLOCATION DENSITY

This is the part where I tell you how handsome he is, your boyfriend, your soon-to-be husband. I don't say this because he is or isn't handsome. It is not about his six and a half feet tall. It isn't about brown eyes or green eyes or the lazy way his lip falls open when he has something to say. This isn't about sex appeal. This isn't about the time you did or did not kiss me in the laundry room (depending on who is speaking; depending on who is listening). This is not about your long brown hair. Or the hot drawl you wanted me to train you out of. This is not about Yankee fixation on the wonders of the new south, the dirty south. This is not about you or me or the man who has you on your hands and knees. This is not about the threesome he hinted about that night on the couch, you sitting between us with your hand on both our knees. This is not about the Julia Roberts movie we made you turn off or the way suddenly I was in charge. This is not about you and it's not about me, it's not even about your boyfriend, however handsome he may be. This is about luck, the last three letters of the alphabet, the sound your mouth makes when it has something in it, and the things he doesn't know.

SLACK LINES

I took a picture of the bed. I know it's sick. The bed we never fucked in. I took a picture of the bed, telephone pole sideways out the window, slack lines in shallow U, the church bells ringing while I took the picture, the steeple out of sight. Your blonde hair. Or was it red then? I took a picture of the bed, messed sheets, the roses dying on the side table, dropping petals on the yellow Westclock with tarnished gold around the edge, tarnished ticking arms that went around ticking, ticking while I watched you sleep, your stomach rising, your stomach falling, your chest rising, your chest falling, and the way your leg kept kicking out, the way I moved to let it touch me.

SAINTLY MEAT OF THE HEART

Grey of rooftop angles fills the window frame. Two panes, painted shut a generation ago. The eave's line cuts a half V across, blocking where the sun wants in. Bright colors of book spines slim in late afternoon. I wanted this. The desert song, long coyote wail. Perhaps the metaphor wants something else.

The first time I cried it was like this. Every other time has been the same caked-on ice melt and shock of weed growth shown through. Shock of silence, tempered by the footfall.

What did you want from me? The goal was not to break glass. We didn't break glass. We didn't break a thing.

BARN SWALLOWS

My sorrow hangs just inside the door. The gate a grey sunset covered in rain. It hollered as I shook it, screeched to let me in. Then wet steps, then lock in the door, key in the lock, curled hand removing the metal C in one flick of the wrist, cracking back. I left the door open because of the dark. The grey birds in the eaves. I swam blurred in orange, in deep red, tears draped over the rusted metal. Then bent sorrow back into darkness when the only bare bulb exploded like a sudden photo shot. I hung onto the walls, afraid of not fearing anymore. When I was done with her, I got into the car and wondered where all the dust on the dashboard came from. How I might more carefully open and close the door to let less in. Or perhaps the dust is me.

The barn looms, like a large adolescent girl, like barns do. I have to go back to make sure I've closed everything tight, the gate, the door, the latch, is the nail in tightly, the one where I hang my coat when I have one, is the other nail in tightly, the one rusting into my sadness. If she falls to the floor there's no telling where she'll end up. My father might see her lying there and throw her away or feed her to the pigs. Grandmother might place her on grandfather's grave. Mother might mistake my sorrow for herself, buy her things, brush the hair she doesn't have, take her tanning, set her up with a boy.

GRAND CANYON

I say wife and my father hears knife. I think it's got something to do with religion. I'm not trying to do this *to* him. I tell him, remember the bad portrait over the single bed in the spare bedroom. Remember the horse's head, the snaking antlers that held hats for you. Your black jacket and the scratchy couch I burned my legs on. Remember the wrong shoes and the miles and miles of trail, the snake, the hill, the white rock that went on forever. Remember the red apple of a child's toy that bumped twice and descended forever. Remember the gallon jug carried into the ravine, small stones pressing into your heel like forever. The empty bottle crushed in next to your spine the whole hike out. Remember your thirst like it was something that mattered.

MATCHES BETWEEN TEETH

You were all summer and I was the hands in your hair. We fished off the yellow pier or, I should say, you fished off the pier while I watched from the trees. You were never me enough but I made do with you. I made us lie side by side mimicking each other's limbs until we were fooled by mirror or fire. I conspired to get you to live with me. I got rid of your mail, I lost your dog, your mother, your shoes, I trained them to love again and then set them all free. You were washing dishes with your back to me, saying something about fireflies or mosquitoes. You told me to shut the screen. I turned your neighbors out of their homes, checked all the attics for sparrows, then set the first blaze.

SOMEWHERE WE BURN

Somewhere we burn, fur-covered, wood smoke and grease stain. Love is never clean like memory. Somewhere ashes scatter. Think of the sea floor, think of every brazen inch of beach, think mountains and where we end up childless in a rocky corner. Rocking chair tears my mother's hand, she bleeds on baby. Think of every last disaster you were part of. Start from the start, make it clean. Make it right. Make it real.

AUTOMATIC COLOR ADJUSTMENT
OF A TEMPLATE DESIGN

It snowed all morning. Rivers of cold wet leapt at our tires. They say 20 miles from here a pile-up killed 14 people, but our roads are clear. In this town nothing stays.

COMMON SAGE

We were all talking about how the world would end. And then it did, air circulating around the ward and resting on the plastic collection of leaves in my grandmother's room, the snipers still on the run and towers smoldering after the fall. You argue about water, misread my spout about natural gas for talking about oil. *I'm done talking about oil*, I say, which you take for victory. You tell me they want the great lakes to drown the southwest with overconsumption. And then there's something about trails and I see the light of the moon filtering through the line a jet has left in the sky. Everything's blue, including your eyes, the bluest, when the ticking finally comes to an end.

FROM NOW

The sky is nothing but blue today, unbroken. It seems to be waiting. Two black birds, three cut through it. Still its attention does not waver. Like a dog waiting for a thrown ball or a woman drained of her options, it will see nothing else. By the time you get back the window will be open, green leaves against the pale, the room empty, the song we both liked will be forced on repeat. Years later you won't remember my name.

2-STEP

You thought a little dancing would do it. Knowing my weakness for the slide guitar, you chose a country station playing classic cowboy songs all night. There were other people there but there weren't other people there. There were moths against the glass wanting to abandon the night for the fiery spark of my thrift store lamp. When we lit cigarettes, we held them away from our faces because they were so close. I could smell your beer breath, a hint of rum, and love you for it the way I could not love you for anything else. I memorized the feel of your wrist, the way it twisted to get out of my grasp during the last long gasp of your hips moving under me. And the song about waltzing across Texas went on forever while the radio died with the last closing door.

APOSEMATIC

In rat colonies, the women don't die. They get stuck on glue traps and dropped out of windows of fifth-floor tenements while foraging for food. Sometimes they don't fade right away. Their little legs break from the fall and they land, belly down on the sticky, their tails flapping around. I've seen it. I've heard the babies crying through walls.

The tarantula hawk wasp dislikes gestation. Blueblack body and rust-colored wings. Whore that she is, swollen belly full of stones. Whore that she is, swollen stinger. Indolent and drunk, rotted fruit on her chest, she fucks her babies into the belly of a lady spider she's convinced to come home. When they wake she's devoured whole as the children dig out, organs fading last in a gasp of desire.

My mother used to bring men home. They'd fuck and fall asleep on the couch. My brother's hollering never woke them up. I wore little to get to the milk in the morning. I wore less when they held me down.

I am going to keep on believing in the devil, until the earth is proven otherwise uninhabitable. The great unimaginable caverns below us are really doorways into our souls. So what's this about the eyes as the windows, cracked, shut, bleeding, smeared with weather and worn. Great untapped mercies live within us.

ABOUT THE AUTHOR

Elizabeth J. Colen lives in the Pacific Northwest. This is her first book.

LaVergne, TN USA
07 June 2010
185251LV00002B/1/P